3/04

SPACE EXPLORATION

Please visit our web site at: **www.garethstevens.com**
For a free color catalog describing Gareth Stevens Publishing's list of high-quality books and multimedia programs, call 1-800-542-2595 (USA) or 1-800-387-3178 (Canada). Gareth Stevens Publishing's fax: (414) 332-3567.

Library of Congress Cataloging-in-Publication Data

Quest.
    Space exploration.
       p. cm. — (Discovery Channel school science. Universes large and small)
      Contents: Space exploration — Wish upon a star — Countdown to the unknown — Back to the future — Out of this world — Man on the moon — Searching the universe for signs of life — Far out: getting there — No weighting — Night watch — Double trouble for the Hubble — ET, where are you? — The truth about Mars — Space lite — Final project: is anybody out there?
      ISBN 0-8368-3373-2 (lib. bdg.)
      1. Outer space—Exploration—Juvenile literature. [1. Outer space—Exploration.] I. Title. II. Series.
QB500.22.Q47 2003
919.904—dc21
                                   2003042498

This edition first published in 2004 by
Gareth Stevens Publishing
A World Almanac Education Group Company
330 West Olive Street, Suite 100
Milwaukee, WI 53212 USA

Writers: Jackie Ball, Paul Barnett, Dan Franck, John-Ryan Hevron, Susan W. Lewis, Diane Webber, Christina Wilsdon, Sharon Yates, Zachary Zimmerman

Editor: Sharon Yates

Photographs: Cover: Hubble Space Telescope, NASA; p. 2, Hubble Space Telescope & galaxies, NASA; p. 3, astronaut, NASA; p. 3, globe, MapArt; pp.4-5, galaxies, NASA; pp. 6-7, star background, © PhotoDisc; pp. 8-9 NASA; p. 10, Galileo's telescope, Scala/Art Resource, NY; p.11 Newton's telescope, ©Royal Greenwich Observatory/Science Photo Library/Photo Researchers; p.11 Keck Telescope, ©Simon Fraser/Science Photo Library/ Keck Observatory/ Photo Researchers; p. 11 Chandra telescope, NASA; p.12, Hubble Space Telescope, NASA; p.13, nebula, NASA; p.13, scale, ©PhotoDisc; p.14-15, Moon landing & Michael Collins, NASA; p. 16, Mars polar ice cap, NASA; p. 17, Stardust spaceship, NASA; p. 22, Debra Fischer, courtesy San Francisco State University; p. 22, telescope & observatory, ©PhotoDisc; p. 23, Maria Mitchell, Maria Mitchell Assn.; p. 24, Hubble Space Telescope, NASA and Hubble (top, right),

This U.S. edition copyright © 2004 by Gareth Stevens, Inc. First published in 2000 as *Quest: The Space Exploration Files* by Discovery Enterprises, LLC, Bethesda, Maryland. © 2000 by Discovery Communications, Inc.

Further resources for students and educators available at www.discoveryschool.com

Designed by Bill SMITH STUDIO
Creative Director: Ron Leighton
Designers: Nick Stone, Sonia Gauba, Bill Wilson, Darren D'Agostino, Joe Bartos, Dmitri Kushnirsky
Photo Editors: Jennifer Friel, Scott Haag
Art Buyers: Paula Radding, Marianne Tozzo

Gareth Stevens Editor: Betsy Rasmussen
Gareth Stevens Art Director: Tammy Gruenewald
Technical Advisor: Russell Berg

Printed in the United States of America

1 2 3 4 5 6 7 8 9 07 06 05 04 03

©PhotoDisc; p. 25, weightlessness, NASA; p. 26, plaque, NASA; p. 26, Carl Sagan, Mikhail Lemkhin/Archive Photos; p. 27, Accibo Puerto Rico Telescope, ©David Parker/Science Photo Library/Photo Reasearchers; p. 29, magnifying glass, ©PhotoDisc; p. 30, toilet, NASA; p. 30, astronaut, ©PhotoDisc; p. 31 scientists, NASA; p. 31, hand computer, Ron Leighton; all other photos are ©COREL.

Illustrations: p. 21, Gary Ciccarelli; p. 26, Sebastian Quigley.

Acknowledgements: pp. 14-15, "Man on the Moon" excerpted from APOLLO 11 LUNAR SURFACE JOURNAL edited by Eric M. Jones, NASA, www.hq.nasa.gov/alsj © 1995, and APOLLO EXPEDITIONS TO THE MOON edited by Edgar M. Cortright, NASA, SP; 350, Washington, D.C.; p. 15, "Space Jitters" excerpted from FLYING TO THE MOON: AN ASTRONAUT'S STORY by Michael Collins, A Sunburst Book (Second Edition), Farrar, Straus & Giroux, Inc., NY, © 1994, 1976; pp. 24-25, background information about the Hubble, ADVENTURE IN SPACE: FLIGHT TO FIX THE HUBBLE by Elaine Scott and Margaret Miller, Hyperion (J), NY © 1995.

Discovery CHANNEL SCHOOL SCIENCE

CONTENTS

SPACE EXPLORATION

We've been on an adventure—all of us on Earth. We used to think our planet, not the Sun, was the center of the universe. We also used to think our Solar System and our galaxy were the only ones in the universe. They are not. There are other planetary systems, other galaxies. Many people still think we are the only intelligent life that exists. Are we? Maybe you will find out in your lifetime.

In SPACE EXPLORATION, Discovery Channel takes you out of this world to discover what we know and how we know it. Some of it is pretty far-out. But two things are certain: The journey is exciting, and, in many ways, the adventure is just beginning.

Why is this astronaut underwater? See page 25.

Final Project

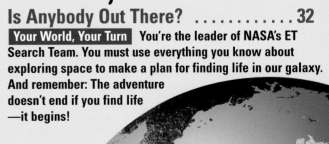

Space Exploration

You can turn on the news several times a year and see a great bird, a space shuttle, being carried into space on an even greater bird, a huge liquid fuel tank and two reusable solid rockets. And yet, it is somehow not surprising that hundreds of years ago, Leonardo da Vinci foresaw this. Humans have always turned their hearts and minds to the vast beyond, using the greatest of all human tools, the imagination.

The photograph you see on this page is of two galaxies nearly colliding, as taken by the Hubble Space Telescope. It is a picture that inspires awe in all of us. Do you think a shepherd felt a similar sense of awe when watching a full eclipse of the moon 3,000 years ago on a dark hillside in ancient Persia? Our quest for knowledge about space is a deep and ancient one. It is shared by all cultures and all ages, those technologically advanced as well as those whose only tools are the stories they tell.

Modern space exploration goes far beyond even the wildest dreams of old. As you read about our modern tools and milestones, keep in mind that there's a whole lot more to discover about the universe. Remember, too, that we stand on the shoulders of giants, or at least dreamers. So, turn the pages and start dreaming.

"The great bird will take its first flight on the back of a great bird . . . bringing glory to the nest where it was born."

—Leonardo da Vinci, 1505

GALAXIES IN MOTION

This spectacular photograph, taken by the Hubble Space Telescope, shows two spiral galaxies almost colliding—but they didn't. Instead, they passed each other in space. Telescopes like the Hubble are our eyes in the sky. They show us what we can't see. Larger than a school bus and weighing over 12 tons (11 tonnes), the Hubble orbits Earth sending us pictures of astounding clarity. Find out more about the Hubble on pages 24 and 25.

Wish Upon A Star

Q: You're Alpha Centauri, the "star" of our show tonight. We have contacted you through a special series of radio wave relays to talk about why people are so fascinated with space. Could you, er, shed some light on the subject?

A: (inaudible)

Q: What's that? We can't hear you. Please speak up.

A: I said, I'm shouting. It's not easy to be heard from 25 trillion miles away. In other words, 43 trillion kilometers. Or put another way, 4.3 light-years. However you want to measure it, it's a long way.

Q: You're trillions of miles away? But your life story says you're the star closest to Earth.

A: Well, that's *almost* true. Your Sun is the star closest to Earth. And Proxima Centauri is actually a fraction of a light-year closer than I am. Big deal. In space that distance is SO nothing, believe me. But I'm just about the closest, and I AM the brightest star in the constellation Centaurus. That's why I'm Alpha—after the first letter of the Greek alphabet. Numero Uno. When it comes to brightness, I get an "A."

Q: Well, good for you. But since you are such an expert, would you mind explaining exactly what a light-year is? Is it a measure of time or light?

A: A light-year is a measure of distance. It's the distance light travels in one year.

Q: But—it doesn't seem as if light takes any time to travel. The Sun shines and we see the sunlight right away.

A: It only seems that way. It actually takes a few minutes for the Sun's light to reach Earth. Light travels at the rate of 186,000 miles (300,000 km) per second, and the Sun is 93 million (150,000 million km) miles away. So do the math. Light is fast, but hey—it can't perform miracles.

Q: You mean to tell us that since you're more than four light-years away, it takes four years for your light to reach the Earth? So when we see you shining—

A: You're looking four years back through time. Yep. Amazing but true. And don't forget, I'm one of the closest stars to Earth. Other stars are millions of light years away from you. So when you see them, you're really seeing ancient history in the making. You could be watching a star being born, or dying. Both events happen all the time. Everything has a life cycle, even the trillions of stars up here.

Q: Are there really trillions of stars out there?

A: At least trillions. You can only see about 4,000 of them with the naked eye, but there are over a hundred billion stars in our own galaxy, the Milky Way, alone. Your Sun, the center of your Solar System, is just one. And there are 50 billion galaxies, and millions of stars in THEM, and . . . well, you get the picture. I come from a very big family.

Q: Are all stars alike?

A: Yes and no. We're all made of the same elements—helium and hydrogen. That includes your Sun, naturally. But we're different temperatures. I mean, we're all superhot—after all, that's what gives us our radiant glow. But some stars are hotter than others. And that affects whether we're blue or red or brown or yellow. So does our age.

Q: Do all stars stay together in galaxies?

A: Mostly. But galaxies are just one grouping. Galaxies themselves are kind of clumped into clusters, which can contain up to thousands of galaxies. Within clusters, galaxies orbit each other at about 500 miles (805 km) per second, held together by gravity. And the clusters are often in superclusters that can be as large as 1 billion light-years across. The Milky Way itself, just one galaxy, is 100,000 light-years across. So you get the picture. Space is BIG. But not crowded.

Q: Why not?

A: Because there's so much empty space between us. Scientists think that as much as 95 percent of the universe is huge, empty space. Voids. So imagine how big the whole thing is.

Q: With all those stars, scientists think there are other solar systems up there. Can you tell us how many?

A: Nope. No can do. That's for me to know and you to find out.

Q: Oh, come on. Please?

A: Sorry. Can't. You gotta find out for yourselves. You've only been doing serious exploration, first with small telescopes, then with more powerful telescopes, and now with probes and space shuttles, for about 400 years. That's not even a blink in space time, and you've already come a long way. Give yourselves a little more time.

Q: Why do you think people keep trying to learn more about space?

A: Why not? It is so gorgeous up here. And so big. Endless. There's so much to explore. Room to roam. Earth people like that concept. You know, "Don't fence me in." You guys spent hundreds of years exploring your planet. But that was nothing next to space.

Q: O.K. Let me just ask you outright: Is there anybody up there?

A: Won't answer. Can't tell. That would take all the fun out of it for you. But I will tell you this: The universe is in a constant state of change. Stars are born and stars die all the time. And any one of those stars could theoretically be the center of a solar system, just like your Sun. So any one of those theoretical solar systems could be like yours. Or very different.

Q: So there could be thousands of other solar systems. Maybe millions. Meaning thousands or millions more planets like Earth. Maybe with people like us on them.

A: Yep. Or there could be different planets with different life-forms. LOTS of different life-forms. So someday you'll have more answers—but never all the answers. That's why you'll always want to keep exploring.

Activity

GET ON BASE Scientists think a lunar base could be established early in the twenty-first century for further exploration of the Moon. What clues would you look for to figure out the Moon's history? Think of atmosphere, water, and land formations.

Countdown to

| **1926** | **1957** | **1969** | **1976** |

We started exploring space from space in 1957. In this short time, there have been many milestones. A few are shown here. But hold onto your space belts! Many more are bound to happen as we continue to explore the unknown.

1926

Robert Goddard, a physicist, fires a small rocket (just 4.5 feet long or 1.5 meters long) from his aunt's farm in Massachusetts, using gasoline and liquid oxygen as fuel. This shows that liquid fuel can power rockets into outer space. Rockets built later in the twentieth century are bigger, but they use Goddard's rocketry principles.

1957

The former Soviet Union launches the world's first satellite, *Sputnik 1*, into orbit around Earth. Its success kicks off the space race between the Soviet Union and the United States in which each country tries to score the most "space firsts." One month later, *Sputnik 2* carries a dog named Laika into orbit, proving a living creature can survive in space. Four years later, Yuri Gagarin, a Russian, becomes the first human in space when he orbits Earth in *Vostok 1.*

1969

On July 20, millions of people around the world turn on their TVs to see a live broadcast—from the Moon. They watch and listen to American astronauts Neil Armstrong and Buzz Aldrin—the first people to walk on a world other than Earth (shown above, left). No signs of life are found then—nor have any been found by the other ten Americans who landed on the Moon in follow-up trips.

1976

Viking 1 (shown below) and *Viking 2* put two landers on Mars to find out if life exists there. The robots do tests of Martian soil. No signs of life are detected, but Mars's surface shows that water once flowed in its channels. Frozen water is discovered at the planet's northern polar cap, raising hopes of finding new clues there in the future.

the Unknown

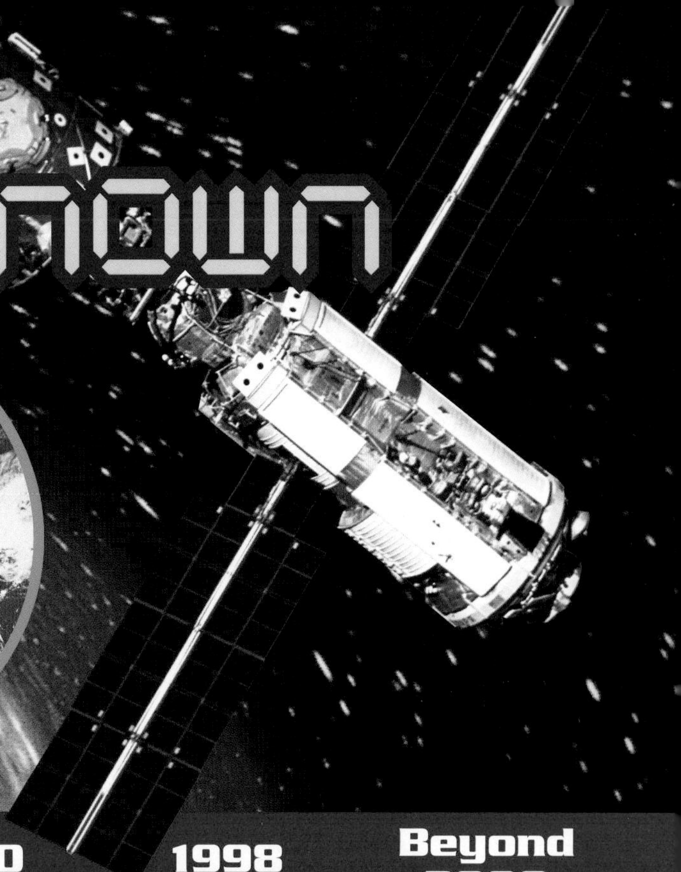

| 1981 | 1986 | 1990 | 1998 | Beyond 2000 |

1981

The *Columbia* (shown below) ushers in the era of the space shuttle, a reusable craft that looks and lands like a plane but flies like a spaceship. But in 1986, the shuttle program suffers a tragic setback when the *Challenger* explodes just after liftoff. It is more than two years before the shuttle program continues. Then in 2003, the *Columbia* breaks apart on re-entry into Earth's atmosphere. In both tragedies, all those aboard died.

1986

Russia launches the Mir Space Station, in which cosmonauts and then American astronauts live and work for months at a time. It is used for the next thirteen years to study the long-term effects of living in space and proves humans are able to live there.

1990

The Hubble Space Telescope (shown above in the circle) is launched into orbit above Earth's atmosphere. It transmits the clearest pictures of things in space because it is beyond the distorting effects of Earth's atmosphere.

1998

The first three sections of the International Space Station (shown above) are linked in orbit. When all twenty-four sections are ready in 2004, the station will be the size of two football fields. People from different nations will live and work there. Others may go for a short visit. Future probes may use it as a launching pad to go deeper into the universe.

Beyond 2000

The first spacecraft to Pluto takes off. It will arrive between 2006 and 2008. More robots land on Mars. *Voyagers 1* and *Voyager 2* travel past our Solar System, carrying messages from Earth. Who knows what or whom they may find?

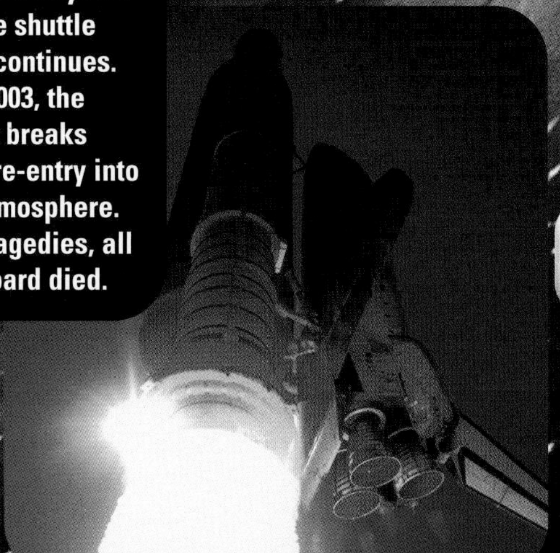

Activity

FUTURE FIRSTS Many firsts in space—from new discoveries to cities and industries located in space—will happen in the twenty-first century. Maybe you will work in space or go there for a summer. Make a list of ten things you think will happen in space by the year 2020. Describe the events and explain why you chose them.

Back to the Future

Before 1957, we were limited to exploring space with telescopes from Earth. A telescope is like a time machine. When you look through it into space, you not only get a close-up picture of objects that may be hundreds of millions of miles away—you also see deep into the past. That's because light takes a long time to travel these huge distances—even though it's whipping along at about 186,000 miles (300,000 km) per second! The Sun's light takes about eight minutes to make the 93 million mile (150 million km) trip to Earth. So you actually always see the Sun the way it looked eight minutes ago! It works the same way with other stars—except now you're talking years, not minutes. Light from Proxima Centauri, the second-closest star to us in our galaxy, takes four years to reach us.

Some of our telescopes are incredibly powerful. They see energy that was given off over 12 billion years ago! That's when the universe was very young. Telescopes are helping us solve the mysteries of our universe—how it formed, if there are other life-forms in it, and what's going to happen to it, and to us, in the future.

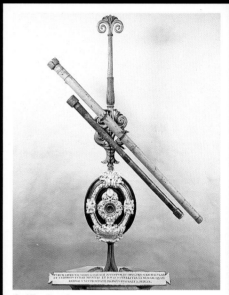

Galileo's telescope

Starry Eyed

Ancient peoples didn't have telescopes, so they relied on their eyesight to study the sky. They observed a lot this way. They picked out constellations among the stars and figured out the motion of the Sun and Moon. They also built stone structures that lined up with the different positions of the Sun, Moon, and sometimes the stars. This one is Stonehenge, built in England nearly 5,000 years ago.

Stonehenge

Seeing Is Believing

How would you like to have a few moons named after you? The four biggest moons of Jupiter are called "Galilean" moons in honor of the first person to see them: the Italian scientist Galileo. Galileo spied these moons in 1610, using a telescope he built himself. It contained two lenses that focused light and made the things he looked at appear thirty-two times larger. It was called a refracting telescope. Galileo was also the first person to see our Moon's mountains and craters.

Galileo's discoveries made him famous, but they also got him into serious trouble. Leaders of the Catholic Church banned his books because they contradicted the Church's teachings. The Church taught that Earth was the center of the Solar System. Galileo was punished because he wrote that Earth revolves around the Sun. He was put under "house arrest" and had to stay inside his home until he died.

No Fuzzies

Even though Galileo was not allowed to leave his house because of his ideas, he continued to write. It's a good thing he did, too. His books were read years later by the English mathematician Sir Isaac Newton and others. Newton is most famous for figuring out the law of gravity and what makes things move. In 1668, he invented a new kind of telescope, one that used mirrors and lenses and made objects appear less blurry. It was called a reflecting telescope, and it paved the way for the big reflecting telescopes we use today.

Newton's telescope

Keck Telescope

Chandra X-ray Observatory Space Telescope

'Scopes in Space

Big telescopes on Earth are great, but they can see only so far. Their view is affected by artificial light, air pollution, and Earth's atmosphere. To get really clear views of what's out there, scientists are sending telescopes into space.

The most famous space telescope is the Hubble, which was launched from the space shuttle *Discovery* in 1990. It orbits Earth at a height of 370 miles (595 km). The Hubble has sent back amazing pictures of Mars and other planets, exploding stars, nebulae, and galaxies as they appeared 10 to 12 billion years ago.

In July 1999, the Hubble was joined in space by the Chandra X-ray Observatory. This telescope "sees" X rays given off by space objects that are billions of light years away. Photographic equipment and computers turn the X rays into pictures for us. In fact, if your sight were as keen as Chandra's, you could read a newspaper headline just one-half inch (1.25 centimeters) high from one-half (.8 km) mile away!

Humongous

Galileo and Newton would probably gasp at the size of our current telescopes. These telescopes can probe very deep into space. The Keck Telescope and its twin, Keck II, are positively gigantic. Each has a big mirror made up of 36 small mirrors and measures about 33 feet (10 meters) wide. They sit near each other atop an unlikely place: the volcano Mauna Kea in Hawaii. But don't worry, the volcano is not active. An electronic link between the telescopes lets them function together as one giant telescope that sees light 14 billion years away.

Hard to believe, but there's an even bigger telescope. It's the Very Large Telescope (VLT) in Chile. This humongous telescope includes four big telescopes and three smaller ones. The mirror in each one is 27 feet (8 m) wide. In 2002, the telescopes will began working together as one.

Activity

SCOPE IT OUT Check in with web sites that monitor the progress of space telescopes. Visit chandra.nasa.gov/chandra.html for news and updates on the Chandra X-ray Observatory. Keep tabs on the Hubble at www.stsci.edu. You can also search the Web for the names of other observatories. Find out if a nearby university or museum has a telescope with public viewing hours.

FAR OUT

The nearest galaxy to us is the Large Magellanic Cloud. It is 170,000 light years away. This means the galaxy's light travels 170,000 years to reach us. In other words, we're seeing the galaxy as it was 170,000 years ago. The further we look into space, the further we look back in time. With space telescopes and probes, we're able to see practically to the beginning of the universe. Looking at a galaxy or at anything else in space is like being in an astronomical time machine! This is how far out some things really are:

Earth to Moon	240,000 miles (385,000 km)
Earth to Sun	93 million miles (150 million km)
Sun to Pluto	3.5 billion miles (5.6 billion km) (average)
Sun to Proxima Centauri (nearest star)	4.2 light-years*
Earth to Large Magellanic Cloud (nearest galaxy)	170,000 light-years*
Earth to Andromeda Galaxy (nearest large galaxy)	2, 200,000 light-years*

*(1 light-year = 5.9 trillion miles; 9.29 trillion km)

Can you express the distance to the nearest galaxy in light-years using scientific notation (powers of ten)?
Check your answer on page 32.

GOBS OF GALAXIES

You're on Earth, and Earth is part of our Solar System. Our Solar System is part of the Milky Way Galaxy. It has over 100 billion stars. That's huge. Now think of the universe. It contains about 50 billion galaxies. That's too huge to imagine. But luckily, the universe is organized in an easy way. Just as the United States is organized into cities, states, and regions, the universe is made up of galaxies, groups of galaxies (clusters), and groups of clusters (superclusters). Here's how you and other Earthlings fit into the picture:

You

Earth

Solar System

Milky Way Galaxy

Local Group Cluster

Local Supercluster

The Universe

GALACTIC GLOBS

A galaxy is a gigantic group of stars, dust, and gas held together by gravity. Galaxies come in three basic shapes. A spiral galaxy is shaped like a pinwheel, with a center and arms swirling around it. Our galaxy, the Milky Way, is a spiral. An elliptical galaxy can be round or egg-shaped. An irregular galaxy is any other shape.

FIND YOUR "WEIGH"

Here's a tricky question:

Q: There is gravity in space. Yes or No?

A: Yes. But what about all those astronauts floating around? Surely that means there's no gravity in space. You're right about that: Space itself has no gravity. But stars, moons, and other planets do. In fact, they have more or less gravity than Earth, depending on their mass. You wouldn't be weightless if you were on another planet, you'd just weigh more or less. See for yourself! Figure out how much you would weigh on each of the planets. Graph your space weights. On which planets would you be lightest? Why?

Planet	Your Earth Weight		Multiply by		Your Space Weight
Mercury	__	X	.38	=	__
Venus	__	X	.91	=	__
Earth	__	X	1.00	=	__
Mars	__	X	.38	=	__
Jupiter	__	X	2.34	=	__
Saturn	__	X	.93	=	__
Uranus	__	X	.79	=	__
Neptune	__	X	1.14	=	__
Pluto	__	X	.04	=	__

YELLOW PAGES TO THE STARS

The Hubble Space Telescope has its own built-in "address book" for 15 million different stars. Each address has the star's exact location so the telescope can find it.

CELESTIAL CONCEPTS

A BLACK HOLE is an area in space packed with very, very dense matter. No light can escape from the area's gravity.

A NEBULA is a cloud of dust and gas.

A SUPERNOVA is a giant star that is exploding and collapsing into its center.

The word **GALAXY** comes from the Greek word meaning "milky." Does the Milky Way look that way to you?

LIFE IN THE SLOW LANE

Did you hear the one about the astronaut who got younger on his space flight? While this sounds like a joke, it also happens to be true! Time slows down when traveling at great speed in space, so space travelers age more slowly than they do on Earth. Albert Einstein figured this out in 1905, long before we started flying in space.

Einstein knew the speed of light never changes—it is constant. This means light always travels at 186,000 miles (230,000 km) per second. Time, however, is relative, said Einstein. It can change. It changes according to the speed of what is measuring it. The faster the speed, the slower time passes. In fact, a very accurate clock aboard a space shuttle was measured after its return to Earth: it lost 0.000,000,000,295 (2.95×10^{-10}) seconds for each second of the trip. Now, this is a very tiny amount to lose, but it proved Einstein's theory. If the shuttle had been traveling near the speed of light and had been gone for several years, the time loss would have been bigger. So, if you went on a very long space trip and your spacecraft could travel close to 186,000 miles (300,000 km) per second, you'd be younger than your current same-age friends when you returned to Earth!

NEW HEIGHTS

Want to get taller real fast? Take a trip to space. Astronauts become 1-2 inches (2.5-5 cm) taller while they're in space. Without Earth's gravity tugging on their bodies, the vertebrae in their spines stretch out. The extra height is only temporary, though. Astronauts shrink back to their normal size after returning to Earth.

Activity

SPACE AGE Can you figure out how much younger an astronaut aboard a shuttle would be if he or she lost 0.000,000,000,295 (2.95×10^{-10}) seconds for each second of a ten-day trip? Hint: It's a very tiny number. Check your answer on page 32.

13

Man on the Moon

I f you dream it, it can happen. President John F. Kennedy dreamed that a person could land on the Moon and return safely to Earth. In 1961, he challenged Americans to make the dream real. Could it be done? No one knew. On July 20, 1969, astronauts Neil Armstrong and Buzz Aldrin walked on the Moon while pilot Michael Collins orbited the Moon in the command module, waiting for them to return. Four days later, they were all safely back on Earth. More than thirty years have passed. No human foot has yet stepped on another planet or moon. But it will happen. People are dreaming of it right now. Maybe that foot will be yours!

Sea of Tranquility, The Moon, July 20, 1969

From the Apollo 11 *command module, astronauts Armstrong and Aldrin crawl through a tunnel to the* Eagle, *the lunar module attached to the command module, to descend to the Moon. At the last minute, Armstrong has to manually steer the* Eagle *away from the planned landing site. It is a rock-filled crater and too unsafe to land there. The module's descent fuel is low—about a minute's flying time left. Armstrong sees a smoother spot nearby and gently sets the* Eagle *down at the Sea of Tranquility. Tune in to the chat with the command center in Houston, Texas:*

Armstrong: Houston, Tranquility Base here. The *Eagle* has landed!

Houston: Roger, Tranquility. We copy you on the ground. You've got a bunch of guys about to turn blue. We're breathing again. Thanks a lot.

Armstrong: Thank you . . . That may have seemed like a very long final phase. The auto targeting was taking us right into a football-field-size crater, with a large number of big boulders and rocks for about one or two crater-diameters around it, and it required flying manually over the rock field to find a reasonably good area.

Houston: Roger, we copy. . . .

Armstrong: We'll get to the details of what's around here, but it looks like a collection of just about every variety of shape, angularity, granularity, about every variety of rock you could find. . . .

Armstrong is first to climb down the ladder from the Eagle *to the Moon's surface.*

I'm at the foot of the ladder. . . . The LM [lunar module] footpads are only depressed in the surface about 1 or 2 inches [2.5–5 cm], although the surface appears to be very, very fine grained. It's almost like a powder. I'm going to step off the LM now.

Armstrong: That's one small step for man; one giant leap for mankind.

He then reports on what the surface soil looks like, how it feels, how it reacts:

. . . the surface is fine and powdery. I can kick it up loosely with my toe. It does adhere in fine layers, like powdered charcoal, to the sole and sides of my boots. I only go in a small fraction of an inch, maybe an eighth of an inch, but I can see the footprints of my boots and the treads in the fine, sandy particles. . . .

Houston: We're copying.

Armstrong: There seems to be no difficulty in moving around as we suspected. It's even perhaps easier than the simulations of one-sixth g [gravity] that we performed. . . . It's absolutely no trouble to walk around.

Armstrong and Aldrin spend 21.6 hours on the Moon and collect 44 pounds (20 kilograms) of stuff to bring home to Earth. After stowing their samples on the Eagle, *they toss their boots, backpacks, empty food containers, and urine bags out of the hatch and* leave them behind on the Moon. The Eagle's ascent rocket blasts them off the Moon for their rendezvous with the orbiting command module. Then they start the journey back to Earth. Michael Collins later recalls:

The first one through the tunnel is Buzz, with a big smile on his face. I grab his head, a hand on each temple, and am about to give him a smooch on the forehead, as a parent might greet an errant child; but then, embarrassed, I think better of it and grab his hand and then Neil's. We cavort about a little bit, all smiles and giggles over our success, and then it's back to work as usual.

Mission complete: Apollo 11 splashes down safely in the Pacific Ocean on July 24, 1969.

"Here Men from the
planet Earth first set foot
upon the Moon, July, 1969 A.D.
We came in peace for all mankind."
—Inscribed on the plaque planted
on the Moon, signed by
the Apollo 11 crew and President
Richard M. Nixon.

Space Jitters

Do you get nervous before being in a school play? Worry you'll make a mistake? You're not alone. Many people do. Astronaut Michael Collins, who flew on Apollo 11, tells us how he felt just before blasting off for the 240,000 mile trip (385,000 km) to the Moon:

Cape Kennedy, Florida, July 1969

"The thing that made our flight different, in addition to the landing itself, was that this was what the whole world had been waiting for. . . . I felt a great pressure on me, a pressure to not make any mistakes, because the whole world was watching. If the crew made mistakes, we would make not only ourselves look ridiculous, but also our whole country.

And, of course, I continued to make mistakes, as all humans do. I remember one night flying . . . over . . . Baltimore and Washington, where I had gone to high school and where my mother still lived. I tried to find my old school and just about had it located when I suddenly realized I wasn't looking at Washington at all, but at Baltimore. Somehow I had turned the two cities around in my mind. And this guy, who couldn't tell Washington from Baltimore when directly overhead, was about to navigate to the Moon and back . . . it made you wonder."

Activity

DESIGN A PATCH Each NASA mission has its own special patch. Astronaut Michael Collins designed this one for Apollo 11. He began by tracing an eagle from a book about birds. What other elements are represented on the patch? Imagine you are a member of the next mission to Mars. Decide on the mission's objectives. Then design a patch for your mission.

Searching the Universe

Is there life anywhere else in space?
If so, what form would it take?
We're just beginning to find some tantalizing clues.

ICE AND BUBBLES

Life, as we know it, needs water to exist. Your body, for example, is 70 percent water. Water makes possible the chemical reactions inside your body's cells that keep life going. That's also true for every other form of life that has ever existed on Earth—from bacteria to beluga whales and daisies to dinosaurs.

And that's why astronomers searching for extraterrestrial life look for signs of water. Although they haven't found liquid water yet, they have found lots of frozen water called "water ice"—at the north pole of Mars, in the atmospheres of Jupiter, Saturn, Uranus, and Neptune, and on the surface of Pluto. Our own Moon, too, seems to have water ice. But the liquid stuff hasn't been flowing like . . . well, water.

Mars Polar Ice Cap

But on March 22, 1998, Earth was hit by the equivalent of a water balloon from space—two meteorites landed in a small town in Texas. They were rushed to a laboratory. A close look at the 4.5-billion-year-old space rocks revealed salt crystals with bubbles of water in them. Are the little drops of water as old as the rocks? Do they come from our Solar System? Or beyond? The bubbles are being studied.

Martians for Real?

Where there's water, there may be life. And Mars has—and had—water. The planet's north pole is covered with frozen water and long channels run across Mars's surface—a pretty good sign that the planet once had flowing, liquid water. And, in 1999, a team of scientists said they found proof that Mars once had a big ocean.

Back in July 28, 1976, Mars gave us a big shock. The *Viking 1* lander, a research robot on Mars, scooped up some Martian dirt and tested it for signs of life. Three tests seemed to show positive results because the soil reacted to nutrients used in the test by producing gases. But scientists concluded the reactions were purely chemical, not indications of life. One reason was because a fourth test did not find any organic carbon, the basic building block of life, in the soil. Some scientists are still hopeful—they think the tests weren't sensitive enough to detect tiny amounts of carbon or that life may be flourishing just a few feet below the surface.

Hidden Oceans?

A little drop of water is a great place to start looking for life. But scientists really want to find big bodies of water. That's why they're studying Jupiter's moons. One of these moons, Europa, may be hiding a salty liquid ocean beneath its frozen surface. Two other moons, Callisto and Ganymede, may also have liquid oceans. If life exists on these moons, it will probably be a simple form of life. Scientists do not expect to be greeted by extraterrestrial octopuses!

← Europa

for Signs of Life

"Spacecraft Stardust"

MEET MY DUST

How did life spring up on Earth over 3.8 billion years ago? According to one theory, it may have come from comets. As a young planet, Earth didn't have lots of water or organic molecules made by living organisms. But it was pounded by comets. Comets are big balls of ice and dust, and they contain water and organic compounds. Maybe comets brought the first seeds of life when they crashed here? Maybe they've planted life on other unknown worlds?

A spacecraft named *Stardust* is now on a 2-billion-mile (3-billion-km) journey to help us find out. *Stardust* is due to meet Comet Wild-2 on January 2, 2004. As it plows through Wild-2's tail of dust and gas, *Stardust* will scoop up tiny pieces and bring them to Earth. The capsule containing the comet dust is scheduled to parachute into Utah at 2:45 a.m. on Sunday, January 15, 2006.

EARTH-SHAKING NEWS!

In 1995, scientists discovered the first planet outside our Solar System—the first clue that our Solar System isn't the only one in the universe. Since then, we have discovered over twenty more of these "extrasolar" planets.

Scientists estimate that one in ten stars in our galaxy alone might have planets orbiting them. If this is true, then the Milky Way holds about ten billion planets—not just the nine in our Solar System. Some of these planets may harbor life. Space may not be such a lonely place after all!

Aliens in Action.

What do we think aliens look like? It's anybody's guess! We often imagine them looking like ourselves, but weird in one way or another. They may be little green people. They may eat strange food, have pointy ears, or speak Klingon as they do in *Star Trek*. Sometimes we picture aliens as nonhuman creatures—plantlike beings or killer buzzards or, as in the TV show "Lost in Space," chimpanzees wearing funny hats. Depending on the story, aliens can be either harmless or dangerous. Here are some from past movies:

- *INVADERS FROM MARS* (1953): They're green—but they're not little! Eight-foot-tall humanlike monsters controlled by a little Martian in a glass ball take over a town.

- *THE BLOB* (1958): Eek! This invader is a slimy, oozing blob that devours any living thing in its path.

- *CLOSE ENCOUNTERS OF THE THIRD KIND* (1977): Aliens are wise, kind beings who only want to make contact with us.

- *STAR WARS* (1977) AND LATER *STAR WARS* FILMS: Aliens of all shapes and sizes appear in the "Star Wars" series, from the sluglike Jabba the Hutt to the teddy-bearish Ewoks.

- *E.T.* (1982): E.T.'s a space alien who is a friendly, funny-looking creature with a fondness for candy.

FAR OUT: GETTING THERE

Cape Canaveral, Florida
Homebase for NASA's space shuttle—the world's first reusable spacecraft.

EQUATOR

Kourou, French Guiana
Talk about international! The European Space Agency—made up of fourteen nations—launches its *Ariane 5* rocket from this center in South America.

Rocket science, once a specialty of the United States and the former Soviet Union only, has gone global. Countdowns to blastoff are spoken in more languages now than ever before.

But some places on this planet are better than others for launching rockets into space. Many of the world's launch centers are located near the equator, where Earth spins fastest on it axis. Why? Imagine a slingshot twirling around your finger. The faster it spins, the faster and further its toy missile goes, right? The same is true for rockets. The extra spin gives rockets extra power to push past the pull of Earth's gravity.

A spacecraft can't blast off without the power of a rocket zooming it upward against the grasping force of Earth's gravity. A rocket gets its power from mixing liquid oxygen and liquid fuel together, a combination that ignites with a "boom." The explosion produces a tremendous amount of energy in the form of gases. The gases are expelled from the bottom of the rocket, with great force, pushing the rocket and its spacecraft up and away. It is the reaction to the force of the gases that causes the lift. For every reaction there is an equal and opposite reaction.

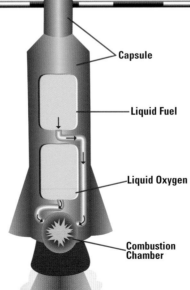

Capsule

Liquid Fuel

Liquid Oxygen

Combustion Chamber

BOOM

ZOOM

Baikonur, Russia The Mir space station went up from here in 1986. It didn't come down until 1999.

Xi Chang Satellite Launch Center, China The Chinese made their first venture into space with the *Mao 1* satellite in 1970. Their current specialty is launching satellites for other nations.

Tanegashima, Japan Japan is the fourth country to make it to space. It builds, tests, launches, and tracks its satellites from this island base.

Sriharikota Launching Range, India In 1980, India became the seventh nation in space when it launched a satellite.

San Marco Launch Platform, Formosa Bay, Kenya Italy's launch pad is the only one in the world located south of the equator.

Rocket Routine In a typical week, two spacecraft are taking off from somewhere in the world. The launch could be an orbiter or probe or shuttle whose mission is scientific observation or exploration. Or a launch could be sending a weather, communications, scientific, or military satellite into orbit around Earth. In the future, spacecraft will be carrying visitors and residents to space stations and cities. What do you think your address would be if you lived in a space city?

Activity

DREAMS ARE REAL Inspired by *Sputnik* in 1957, Homer H. Hickam, Jr., a West Virginia teenager, became fascinated with rockets. With the support of his science teacher and three pals, Homer built and tested a series of rockets, overcoming many obstacles along the way. This story was told in a 1999 movie called *October Sky* and is based on Homer's book about his life, entitled *Rocket Boys.* Today, Homer trains astronauts at NASA. His dream came true. Read the book or rent the video. Then write an essay about your dream and how you think you can make it come true for you.

No Weighting

YOU still don't know exactly how it all happened. You were walking down the street and noticed a huge travel poster advertising "Out of This World Vacation Packages." Suddenly, you were wearing a shiny padded suit that seemed to weigh as much as the contents of your whole closet . . . maybe your whole house. You tried to protest, but your head was enclosed in a clear, hard bubble, so nobody could hear you. You remember seeing a sleek white spacecraft and then climbing some sort of ladder and being strapped into a seat. And before you could say "blast off!" you were doing just that. Or rather, your spacecraft was. The powerful rockets driving the craft roared as their load of liquid fuel and liquid oxygen ignited. The cabin trembled violently as the explosion spewed out gas and vapors.

YOU were afraid your teeth might shake right out of your skull as up, up, up the rockets propelled the craft. At the same time, what felt like an enormous invisible hand was slamming you back into your seat, pressing you down, down, down. A force equal to the rocket's mighty blast was pushing on you. Your ship was traveling fast, straight up from Earth's surface. Eight or nine minutes later, the pressure on you became less and less. By then your ship had taken you 70 miles (113 km) above Earth.

And now it's quiet. The shaking has stopped. The main engines must have turned off. You're going into orbit, and something is floating in front of you. No! They're your own hands!

Whew! They're still attached but sticking straight out in front of you. Wait a minute. Your hands aren't the only things floating in air. Your whole body has been unbuckled and you're rising like a genie released from a bottle, suspended above your seat. In free fall. Weightlessness.

YOU tumble through the air. You feel light as a feather! Free as a butterfly! On top of the world! Ready to throw up. You're overcome with a seasicky, sickening sort of dizziness. You grab a barf bag out of a dispenser as you read a sign stuck to a wall, explaining that two-thirds of first-time space travelers vomit when they go into free fall. One of the astronauts' training vehicles is even nicknamed the Vomit Comet. The problem? Without the familiar anchor of gravity, your body gets confused. Tiny motion detectors in your inner ears, parts of something called the vestibular system, can't do their job, which is to tell your brain what's up and what's down. But your eyes still know what's ceiling and what's floor. This conflict between your eyes and vestibular system is a large part of what's making you feel sick.

But you don't have time to worry about warring systems. Other weird stuff is happening. Without gravity pulling down, blood and fluids flow up to your head, making it feel like a balloon about to pop. As you float by a metal wall panel, you see a reflection you hardly recognize. The spacesuit and helmet have been somehow removed, and a distorted version of your own face stares back. Puffy eyelids, swollen cheeks. Your floating image is taller than usual, too. Without gravity constantly yanking on your backbone, it's stretched out like an overused rubber band.

YOU start to relax, despite everything. This is really fun. You're getting used to all these strange sensations. You explore the different parts, or modules, of the shuttle. You try out a treadmill after reading that spending time in space results in lost muscle tone, especially in the lower legs. Without gravity to overcome, the muscles simply have less to do. You grab a plastic bag from the wall where it's attached by Velcro, poke it with a needle, shoot hot water into it, and then enjoy a delicious lunch of freeze-dried tuna noodle casserole. You sip water through a straw that you need to keep pinching closed. Without gravity to pull it back, the water would keep on flowing.

And then one last sign says your mission has almost been accomplished and points you in the direction of the shuttle's big rounded windows. You gasp and stare at a sky glowing with light—brilliant stars gleaming red, blue, and yellow; clouds of glowing dust you know are nebulae. Amazing. Gorgeous. Incredible. Then you're back in the suit, strapped into your seat, preparing yourself to re-enter the place where gravity rules. Vacation at the beach will never be the same.

Activity

My Space Place This trip was imaginary, but in your lifetime, space travel may be much more available and affordable than it is now. So you may indeed vacation on a space shuttle or space station—maybe spending months or even years in space. What would you need to feel at home in space? Keep space's special conditions and requirements in mind as you pack your bag and make a plan to stay on a space station for an extended time.

NIGHT WATCH

The tools for sky-watching have changed in the past 150 years, but the way people use them to identify new objects in space has not.

SEE IF YOU CAN SOLVE THIS RIDDLE:

No new planets have been found in our Solar System since the discovery of Pluto in 1930. In the years since you were born, however, the total number of known planets has more than tripled. How can this be?

THE ANSWER: Most scientists believe the nine planets orbiting our Sun are all the planets in our Solar System. So astronomers are looking for and finding "extrasolar planets"—planets beyond our Solar System.

San Francisco, California, 2000

Extrasolar planets are not visible to us on Earth. Our telescopes simply aren't powerful enough to see such far-out planets because planets don't radiate their own light. But we can see the light of the stars they orbit.

To find new planets, some astronomers study wobbles in a star's movements, which might be caused by a planet's gravity pulling on it.

The Planet Search team at San Francisco State University began hunting for new planets more than a decade ago. At first, progress was slow—so slow that astronomers at one meeting laughed when they learned how long it took to process the data. But computers are much faster now. Since the discovery of the first extrasolar planet in 1995, more than twenty

others have been found. "Everywhere we look," reports Planet Search astronomer Debra Fischer, "we find planets."

To carry out the search, Fischer spends several nights a month at Lick Observatory, near San Jose, California. In the afternoon, she sets up the equipment and runs telescope tests. She begins observing stars as the Sun sets; when dawn breaks, she grabs some sleep. Between telescope sessions, Fischer analyzes the data and looks

Debra Fischer

for wobble patterns that might be clues of a nearby planet. "Discovery these days comes while you are looking at computer data," says Fischer, "not images through a telescope."

The Planet Search team made headlines in 1999, when Fischer and her colleagues discovered not just a new planet, but a new planet system. Several years earlier, they had detected a planet orbiting the bright star known as Upsilon Andromedae. But Upsilon Andromedae had an extra wobble. After many more observations, the Planet Search team concluded that three large planets circle Upsilon Andromedae—making it a system of planets like ours! Planet Search announced their discovery together with a Harvard-Smithsonian team, which had also discovered the planets.

Fischer is now searching for more planets orbiting other stars. There are billions of stars in the universe. Maybe she and others will find more planetary systems. Their chances are good and are getting better all the time as our telescopes and computers become more powerful.

The more planets that are found, the more likely it is that some will have just the right conditions for sustaining life. Important discoveries always lead to new questions—and ultimately, to new discoveries.

Before computers were invented, astronomers hunted for planets by comparing photographs taken through telescopes. Planets move along a specific path as they orbit the Sun. Their movement can be tracked by checking different locations on different nights. A special microscope-like device, called a blink-comparator, made comparisons easier. As the device switched between two photos, objects in different locations appeared to blink. Comparing a single pair of photographs required looking at thousands and thousands of stars—and a lot of patience.

Clyde Tombaugh was an amateur astronomer who was searching for another planet in the neighborhood of Neptune. He analyzed photographs day after day, week after week, for ten months. One astronomer told him that he was wasting his time. "If there were any more planets to be found," the astronomer said, "they would have been found long before this." He was wrong. In February 1930, Tombaugh spotted a small object shifting back and forth in the blink-comparator. He had discovered the ninth planet in our Solar System, Pluto.

MARIA MITCHELL

When she was still a teenager, Maria Mitchell helped her father study the stars. Their observation post was the rooftop of their house in Nantucket, an island off the coast of Massachusetts, and their telescope was just four inches long.

One night in 1847, when Maria was 29, she saw a star near the North Star where none had been before. The next night the star had moved to a different spot. Because stars don't move, Maria knew she had discovered a comet. Comets were not rare in those days, but female astronomers were. A year later, she became the first female member of the American Academy of Arts and Sciences. This was a great honor. It took 90 years before another woman was asked to join.

Activity

STARRY SKIES Study the stars every clear night for two weeks and keep a record of how far a star, constellation, or the Moon has moved since your last observation. How will you measure? Compare your first and last measurements. Go out a month after you began and compare again.

DOUBLE TROUBLE FOR THE HUBBLE

If you had a brand-new camera that took fuzzy pictures, you'd probably take it back to the store for a refund or return it to the manufacturer for repair. But what if your new gadget was 380 miles above Earth, took almost ten years to build, and cost $1.6 billion? This was NASA's (National Aeronautics and Space Administration) dilemma after the Hubble Space Telescope was launched in 1990 from the space shuttle *Discovery*. Images transmitted to Earth from the telescope were blurry, when they should have been ten times sharper than any Earth-bound telescope.

The cause was a tiny mistake in the main light-gathering mirror: it was too flat—1/50 the width of a human hair too flat. That's a very, very tiny mistake, but one that turned out to be very important. There were other problems on the telescope, too.

For help, NASA turned to a team of engineers and scientists. They made a series of thumbnail-size mirrors that corrected the problem the same way glasses correct a person's vision, and they figured out solutions for some other problems.

Then it was up to a crew of seven astronauts to fly up to the Hubble on a space shuttle and repair the telescope in space. This was one of the toughest jobs ever given to a shuttle team. It would mean completing five space walks, each one six hours long. No one had ever done this before. It would mean moving huge pieces of equipment in space and disconnecting delicate electronic equipment. It would also mean working very carefully and neatly. A loose screw or piece of space trash could damage the telescope while its insides were exposed during the repairs. And the astronauts would have to do this extraordinarily difficult work while braving -300° F (-184° C) temperatures, zero gravity, and wearing bulky gloves and space suits. Could they do it?

To prepare for the mission, the crew trained hard for ten months. They spent a total of four hundred hours underwater in a weightless-simulation tank —sometimes seven hours at a time—to condition themselves for the space walks. They also practiced using one hundred different kinds of tools. They did three "dress rehearsals" of the mission to make sure they would get it right. It's a good thing they did. During one rehearsal, when the temperature was as cold as it is in space, an astronaut's hand became frostbitten (it healed unharmed). Because of this problem, an extra layer of insulation was added to the astronauts' gloves.

Despite the hard training the astronauts did, NASA believed they would be able to finish only half the repairs. But NASA was in for a big surprise. The astronauts did all the repairs in their eleven-day mission. Since then, the Hubble has sent thousands of beautiful images of the universe back to Earth. Further repairs were conducted in late 1999.

NEARLY NO GRAVITY

Movies often show astronauts bouncing around in a zero gravity training center as they practice how to adjust to the weightlessness of space. Unfortunately for anyone who has ever dreamed of floating in a zero gravity chamber, such places don't exist. Zero gravity cannot be created on Earth for long periods of time.

Instead, astronauts experience weightlessness using other methods. One way is in a 35-foot- (11-m-) deep pool of water called the Weightless Environment Training Facility. The Hubble rescue crew practiced repairing the telescope on a model in this pool. Astronauts wore training versions of their space suits.

Something that looks like a huge air-hockey table helped them practice moving large objects in space. The astronauts were strapped into harnesses and suspended above a floor from which jets of air flowed.

Hubble's Fantastic Finds
Some top discoveries made by the Hubble:

▶ Identified gas whirlpools that can be trapped only by the power of a black hole's gravity—more proof that black holes exist.

▶ Detected oxygen in the atmosphere of Europa, one of Jupiter's moons.

▶ Found ancient helium between galaxies and calculated the speed at which stars and galaxies are moving. Findings support the Big Bang theory, which says a big burst of energy was released in a single explosion between 12 and 14 billion years ago. It also suggests the universe is expanding and pushing galaxies farther apart.

▶ Observed dust clouds that could be newly born solar systems. If they are, there are many more planets out there and many more chances of finding life elsewhere.

Need For Speed
The Hubble speeds around Earth at 5 miles (8 km) per second. If you could drive a car from New York City to Los Angeles at this speed, you'd arrive in California in just 10 minutes!

Activity
HUBBLE'S VISION Edwin Hubble had a lot of theories about the universe, which the telescope named in his honor later confirmed. Look up and read about Edwin Hubble. Compare his theories with what the telescope has discovered. Write a list of any similarities you find.

ET, WHERE ARE

Astronomer Carl Sagan had a lifelong sense of wonder about the universe, and he was always very enthusiastic about sharing this wonder with others. Sagan wrote more than twenty books and was the well-known host of a popular series called *Cosmos,* shown on public television in the 1980s. On this show, Sagan was the audience's tour guide to the universe, explaining astronomy

and space science in ways everyone could understand.

Sagan traced his interest in science back to a visit to the 1939 World's Fair in New York, where "The World of Tomorrow" was the theme. It fascinated the five-year-old kid from Brooklyn, New York. Years later, it was Sagan's own work about astronomy—and the search for extraterrestrial life in particular—that fascinated children and adults alike.

Carl Sagan believed Earth was just one planet and the Sun just one star in a universe that may have 100 billion galaxies and 10 billion trillion stars. He said the word *billion* so many times that TV comedians imitated him, saying *billions and billions.* But Sagan never used that term. "For one thing," he wrote, "it's too imprecise. How many are 'billions and billions'? A few billion? Twenty billion? A hundred billion?" But people liked the term and it stuck to Sagan. Eventually, he gave in to it. "For a while . . . I wouldn't utter or write the phrase, even when asked to. But I've gotten over that. So, for the record, here goes: 'billions and billions.'"

To Sagan, it was logical to assume that in a universe so large there must be other planets where intelligent life has evolved. He helped persuade scientists to use Earth's large radio telescopes to listen for signals from life

Message to ETs

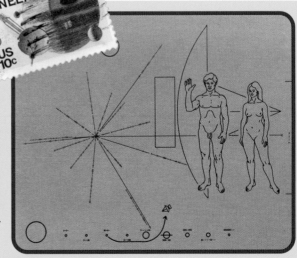

The probes *Pioneer 10* and *Pioneer 11,* launched in 1972 and 1973, both carry the space-age equivalent of a message in a bottle. The two crafts explored Jupiter and Saturn, respectively, and then left our Solar System going in opposite directions. It was Carl Sagan's idea to bolt a gold-plated plaque (shown at right) to each of them for any ET who might see it in the next 100 million years or so. The plaques show Earth's position in the Solar System; the Sun's relationship to other stars; a diagram of a hydrogen atom; and a sketch of a man and woman standing next to the probe.

You?

beyond Earth. More than anyone else, Sagan took the idea of extraterrestrial life out of the realm of science fiction and made it a respected subject for scientific investigation.

Sagan helped NASA plan the *Mariner* spacecraft missions to explore Venus and Mars. "For me, it was just a dream come true," Sagan said. "We were actually going to go to the planets!" These probes discovered that Venus was way too hot to support life and Mars way too cold. Before the *Mariner* probes, scientists thought Venus was cold and Mars hot. Sagan had hoped the probes would find signs of life on these planets, but they did not. Future probes may. Sagan also helped NASA place messages aboard the *Pioneer* and *Voyager* probes, explaining who we are and where our planet is in the Solar System.

Until the end of his life—he died in 1996 at age 62—Carl Sagan hoped we would find signs of extraterrestrial intelligence. He worried that people were believing too much in popular fantasy stories, such as those about alien abductions, and ignoring actual research. "There's so much in real science that's equally exciting [and] more mysterious . . . ," Sagan wrote, "as well as being a lot closer to the truth."

You Can Listen for ETs!

More than a million home computer users are helping scientists listen for messages from extraterrestrials—and you can, too. Here's how it works: The radio telescope at Arecibo, Puerto Rico, is scanning the sky for signals, collecting huge amounts of data. Most of the data comes from Earthlings, but it's possible that some very weak, unusual signal may turn out to be from an extraterrestrial source.

All of the data has to be analyzed—and that's a huge job. SETI (the Search for Extraterrestrial Intelligence) Institute figured out how computer users can help. At www.seti.org/seti/other_projects/seti_at_home.html, you can download software allowing your computer to analyze small parts of the Arecibo data every time it goes into a screen-saver mode. When your computer finishes analyzing a batch of data, it sends the results to SETI@home and gets another. To participate, you must have Internet access and time when *your* computer can be connected to the Internet while data is being transferred. For more information, check out the SETI Institute at www.seti-inst.edu. If you're lucky, it could be <u>your</u> computer that's the first to detect a message from ETs

Activity

EARTH'S GREATEST HITS Carl Sagan headed the committee that decided what was to be included on the gold-plated copper phonograph records attached to the *Voyager 1* and *2* probes that were launched in 1977 and destined to go beyond our Solar System. Each craft carries one record and instructions about how to play it with a needle that is provided. On the record are 115 pictures, messages spoken in 55 different languages, and 90 minutes of music. If you had Carl Sagan's job now, what would you choose? Make a list and compare your selections with those of your classmates. Give the reasons for your selections.

Felix and I sure were lucky! Felix is my best friend. We registered together for the fall 2099 term at the All-Star Space School, but they rarely pick two kids from the same district. We tried to be casual about the obvious competition between us, but deep down we knew the outcome would change things. Solular phones just don't take the place of shooting hoops with a pal. But we were both picked! Far out!

I found Felix shortly after arriving. "Hey Mark, let's go sign up for the Solar Express to Mars," he urged. The trip was at the end of the school term, so I asked him what the rush was for.

"It's really hard to get a slot on the ship," he yelled as he took off down the hall. "You get your own solarvision set and solar station player. And the frozen hot chocolate is free." I caught up to him at the bulletin screen. He was breathing hard from the run, but I still heard him as he whispered in my ear. "There's only room for 20 kids, so you have to get a spot on the list and pass the test."

Just then, two older kids rounded the corner. The taller one scowled as Felix and I punched our ID codes into the screen. He strode up to me followed by his friend who was covered with freckles.

"Planning on going somewhere?" the tall guy asked. His tone had a sarcastic edge.

Felix spoke up loudly. "We've signed up for the Solar Express to Mars." He pointed to the bulletin screen. Our ID codes occupied the last two slots.

"So, you want to go to Mars, huh?" the tall guy sneered, leaning over us. "I went last year, and let me tell you, it's not for little kiddies like you. Why don't you zap those codes and stick to things you'll enjoy, ha, ha."

"I think we'll have a great time," I replied. "We can handle it."

"Okay," the freckled one chimed in. "Let me tell you exactly why you don't want to

go. First of all, the launch pad's not here. You'll be transported to the pad in the Arctic. It's state of the art, but man, it's cold. You'll train there for the final week, and you can't go outside because your nose will freeze and break off. No one wants to see that, right? And when you get to Mars, there's nothing but red sand on the entire planet. It's dry as a bone."

"Plus, you'll weigh almost three times as much on Mars as on Earth," the tall guy interrupted. "Because of the difference in gravity. You'll hardly be able to move. Maybe you'll even get stuck there!"

"Yeah, well, we'll deal," Felix replied. "I'm looking forward to the cool navigational stuff we'll practice on the way to Mars."

Freckles spoke up. "Prepare to be disappointed then," he said with a big smile. "You'll be relying on data from orbiting telescopes, like the Hubble 4

and the Great Raysoscope. The images from those things are the pits. Like looking out of a window that hasn't been cleaned since the last century. You'll have to chart three extrasolar planets. Can you imagine trying to detect the tiny wobble of a star with those telescopes? I'd much prefer to use a VLT-type telescope like the one they have here at school. Then you'll have fun plotting courses instead of frying your eyeballs."

Felix looked shaken. "The Mars trip sounded like so much fun. Now I don't know if I want to go. Maybe we should take our names off the screen."

"Yeah," the tall guy said, "that would be a good idea. Leave the Mars trip to pros like us who've built up a tolerance for this kind of thing."

Felix looked to me with a question in his eyes.

"Don't listen to these guys," I told him. "They don't know what they're talking about. It's obvious they've never been to Mars. Let's go grab some grub, and I'll give you four reasons why I know."

"You're on," he shouted, and took off for the cafeteria. Felix likes to run a lot.

"That was a nice try," I told the two guys. "But next time you should do your homework." Then I ran after my buddy.

What are the four things Mark told Felix in the cafeteria?

Clues

- There's a good reason why launch pads are located where they are.
- Earth's North Pole and Mars's North Pole are both made of this.
- Sometimes less is better.
- Earth's atmosphere surrounds the planet.

(Check your answers on page 32.)

SPACE LITE

SUITED UP

How long does it take you to get dressed in the morning? If you're speedy, maybe about three minutes? It takes an astronaut 45 minutes to put on the 280-pound space suit, including the bulky backpack. Of course, it hardly weighs anything once the astronaut is up in space.

FAST FOOD

Before John Glenn orbited Earth in 1962, scientists didn't know how weightlessness might affect swallowing food while in space. Without Earth's gravity, perhaps food wouldn't move downward in the body. Fortunately, this turned out not to be a problem. But early astronauts were still limited to "safe" foods: bite-size chunks, freeze-dried foods, and gloppy semi-solid food stuffed into toothpaste-like tubes.

Over time, foods and menus improved. Today's shuttle astronauts choose their own menus well before flight time. There's a water dispenser and an oven aboard the craft. All food is ready to eat, or precooked, or made edible by adding water and heating it—just like food you might use on an overnight camping trip. Stowed food must weigh as little as possible to avoid unnecessary weight on the craft during liftoff and flight time. A ready-to-eat meal can be prepared in five minutes; one that requires adding water and heating takes about 30 minutes. Astronauts eat from trays, similar to TV dinner trays.

SPACE TOILETS

Do you know the question astronauts get asked most often? It's: How do you go to the bathroom in space? There is a toilet on the shuttle. Astronauts strap themselves to it so they won't float off. Water isn't used to flush waste products away because it doesn't flow in weightlessness. Air is used instead. It sucks the waste away just like a vacuum cleaner. Solid waste is collected and disposed of back on Earth. Urine is held in a tank, then released into space. The temperature of space is so cold that the urine freezes immediately into sparkling ice crystals. Perhaps some UFO sightings were really Urine Floating Outside!

WHAT'S IN A NAME?

- The Space Shuttle *Endeavour* was named after Captain Cook's ship, which sailed around the world in 1768 while charting Venus's path in the sky.

- The *Enterprise,* the model shuttle that was never flown, was named after the spaceship in *Star Trek.*

- The *Columbia,* the *Apollo 11* craft that carried Neil Armstrong, Buzz Aldrin, and Michael Collins to the Moon in 1969, was named after Christopher Columbus.

LUNAR HUMOR

Why couldn't the astronauts land on the moon?

It was already full.

Why do astronauts like to blast off at noon?

It's launch-time.

What kind of ticks are on the moon?

Luna-ticks!

IMAGINE THAT!

"We know all that the mathematical sciences, astronomy, geology, [and] optics can tell us about the Moon. But no one has ever established direct communication with her," said the president trying to convince the public to pay for a trip to the Moon. This wasn't President Kennedy in the 1960s. This is a fictional character in the 1865 book, *From the Earth to the Moon*, by Jules Verne. *An amazing detail*: Verne's *Columbiad* spaceship was shot from a huge cannon in Tampa, Florida. That's just a few miles (km) from the Kennedy Space Center, where the first real *Apollo* spaceship was launched to the Moon more than one hundred years later.

MIND YOUR METRICS

Mars Climate Orbiter

A simple mistake about a number being metric or imperial caused the Mars Climate Orbiter to disappear in space in 1999. Scientists thought the number they were calculating was metric. It wasn't. The error put the spacecraft only 60 miles (96 km) off course—out of 416 million miles (669 million km) in total—but this little bit meant a lot. The orbiter missed its destination with Mars and was lost in space.

KNOCK, KNOCK, WHO'S THERE?

When astronauts are working in space outside their craft and want to talk to each other without using their radios, they knock their helmets together. Why? Sound waves can't travel in the "nothingness," or vacuum, of space. They need air, or some other matter, to vibrate against.

DAILY DATA

Each day, the Hubble Space Telescope collects enough data to fill an encyclopedia. The data travels more than 90,000 miles (144,810 km) over satellite and ground links before it reaches the Space Telescope Science Institute in Baltimore, Maryland.

Is Anybody Out There?

Today, Planet Earth is the only world we know where life exists. This fact may very well change in your lifetime. New discoveries keep piling up to indicate there may be many, many more places where life can exist than we had ever imagined—not just in our Solar System, but in other planetary systems and in other galaxies. What form would life in other places take? Do you think it will be simple one-celled creatures or some type of intelligent life with which we can communicate? Or both? Or anywhere in between?

Lots of questions. No answers. Yet. In a few years, you and your friends will be in charge of the world (this world, at least). More planetary systems will have been discovered. How should we explore them for signs of life?

Imagine you are at NASA's office on the International Space Station and are leading NASA's ET Search team. Your boss asks you for a plan to explore our galaxy, the Milky Way, for signs of life. The plan has to answer these questions:

- Where will you search—in our Solar System or beyond? Or both?

- How will you search?

- What kinds of vehicles and instruments will you need? What will you look for? What kinds of tests will you use? What will you do if you find signs of life? What will you do if you find intelligent life?

Gather your team and design a plan to answer each of the questions. Then make a poster board display with your plan on it for each question.

Here are some imaginary facts you can assume:

1. **Warp speed:** Spacecraft can fly nearly at the speed of light (186,000 miles or 300,000 km per second).

2. **Space age:** Space explorers traveling at warp speed age about 50 percent slower than their counterparts on Earth.

3. **A Galacta-scope:** A telescope that can detect visible and invisible light rays up to 100,000 light-years away. This just happens to be the diameter of the Milky Way

4. **Space cities:** Earthlings are living in cities in space. (And yes, kids do get homework! And no, no aliens as teachers!)

ANSWERS

Almanac, Far Out, p.12: 1.7×10^5

Almanac, Activity, p.13:
0.00025 second lost.

Solve-It-Yourself Mystery, p. 28–29

1. A real "state of the art" launch center would be close to the equator, where Earth spins fastest on its axis, not at the North Pole where the spin rate is much slower. See Map, p.18.

2. All of Mars is not dry. The north pole is covered with ice. See Searching the Universe for Signs of Life, p. 16.

3. You would weigh less on Mars, not more, because of the difference in gravity. You can calculate what your Martian weight would be by using the chart on p.13 called "Find Your 'Weigh'."

4. While Earth-based reflecting telescopes, such as the VLT (Very Large Telescope), are quite powerful, the images they receive are fuzzy from passing through Earth's atmosphere. Orbiting telescopes, such as the Hubble, are beyond Earth's atmosphere and therefore receive clearer images. See Double Trouble for the Hubble, p. 24.